The Landscape of AVEBURY

Photographs by Bob Croxford

Avebury Henge with its vast circular bank and ditch and huge standing stones is one of the most important prehistoric sites in Europe. It lies in a landscape of equally impressive sites of interest. In this small area can be found Silbury Hill, Europe's largest prehistoric man-made mound and West Kennet, the largest barrow alongside many other remnants and structures from thousands of years ago. The landscape has played a part in the lives of people throughout history. More recently men have used the chalk downs for creating symbolic horses and the fields under the downs have become a centre for the phenomenon of crop circle formations.

Published by Atmosphere
Willis Vean
Mullion Cornwall TR12 7DF
England
Tel 01326 240180
email info@atmosphere.co.uk

ISBN 0 9543409 1 4

Printed and bound in Italy

Frontispeice   Aerial view of AVEBUF

Stone in the AVENUE

Tumuli on a ridge towards FYFIELD DOWN

Winter on the Ridgeway at HACKPEN HILL

Winter inside the south west sector at AVEBURY

THE AVENUE

THE COVE at dawn showing the recently straightened male sto

THE COVE at dawn showing the male stone leaning at eighteen degrees

Stone alignment in the Southern Inner Circle

The North West sect.

Sheep graze inside the Henge and Circle at A\

Part of the South West Sector

Part of the Southern Inner Cir

The SWINDON STONE weighs more than a modern truck

When Alexander Keiller re-erected the BARBER'S STONE the body of a barber-surgeon was found beneath it

The south west section of the AVEBURY HENG

Tree roots on the Henge at the eastern entrance

The South East Sector of the AVEBURY HENG

Sheep are used to crop the grass in the twenty seven acre enclosure of AVEBURY

An old barn inside the Henge

On WINDMILL HILL above the Avebury Henge lies the remains of a banked settlement

WINDMILL HILL commands panoramic views in all directions

SILBURY HILL from the air

SILBURY HILL rises 130 feet above ground level

The shape of the excavated area around SILBURY HILL creates a sensuous landscape

WEST KENNET Long Barrow

Concrete posts mark where the post holes of a vast wooden structure once stood at THE SANCTUARY

On the edge of a field sits the Dolmen called THE DEVIL'S DEN

The view from ADAM'S GRAV

EAST FIELD looking north toward the chalk ridge beyond which is the vale of Avebury

Sunset at OLIVER'S CASTLE

he impressive bank and ditch of THE WANSDYKE was built in Saxon times

The modern horse above DEVIZES was created in 2000

CHERHILL

The CHERHILL WHITE HORSE strides proudly across chalk downs

The ALTON BARNES WHITE HOR…

A Crop Formation in a field below the ALTON BARNES WHITE HORSE   55

Crop formations take many shapes and styles

crop formation close to SILBURY HILL

Some crop formations can only be seen from the air

The timless landscape of the AVEBURY plain is flooded in win

AVEBURY HENGE

Over 5,000 years ago the people of this area started digging a ditch. Their motive remains unclear. The shape is not quite circular but appears to be four separate crescents facing inwards on an area of about 27 acres. Using only the tools of the time, deer antlers as picks and cattle shoulder blades as shovels, they dug and moved 120,000 cubic metres of material. What they dug was not the loose friable chalk you can see on the surface but hard packed solid matter. This was an immense undertaking by any measure, taking about 1,500,000 man

hours. Given enough workers this could have been carried out in a relatively short period of time. This suppose that there were sufficient other workers to provide food, sustenance, shelter and other support. Increasing th time would take it into many seasons. At an outside estimate, from first to last, work was done on the ditch, bar and entrances over a period of 600 years. Because of the short human life-span at that time this approached 35 generations of common endeavour. This is comparable with modern mankind embarking on a project for completion in over a thousand years time. Towards the end of the ditch and henge works 4685 years ago, the first of the immense stones forming the circles was moved into place. The stones were brought from Fyfield Downs about two miles away. Although the stones were not shaped by man they were obviously chosen for certain symbolic importance. The bulging diamond shaped stones are thought to have female attributes while the thinner slender stones are male.

THE WEST KENNET AVENUE

Two rows of standing stones lead from the Sanctuary to Avebury

TREE ROOTS ON THE HENGE

These roots are reputed to have inspired JR Tolkein to write Lord of the Rings

THE COVE

The two stones are thought to have been the entrance to a sacred spot

SILBURY HILL

The largest prehistoric man-made mound in Europe

THE BARBER'S STONE

When this stone was re-erected the skeleton of a barber-surgeon was found underneath

WEST KENNET LONG BARROW

This huge bank and ditch encloses an area of 27 acres

WEST KENNET LONG BARROW

The largest long barrow in England at 107 metres stands on a hill above the River Kennet. Dug from two ditches ten metres either side it encloses five stone-lined chambers made from sarsen boulders. It was used as a ritual burial place for many centuries before being closed and sealed by huge stones.

WINDMILL HILL

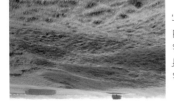

Located approximately one mile north of Avebury, WINDMILL HILL was the site of a 'causewayed enclosure' settled many years before Avebury itself was built. This hilltop gathering place of neolithic traders and early farmers is encircled by three rings of concentric ditches. Excavations in the 1920s found vast quantities of animal bones, worn and broken tools of bone and antler, beads and trinkets and some human remains.

SILBURY HILL

Europe's largest prehistoric earth mound has no conceivable function to modern eyes. At 39 metres high it has a similar mass to Egypt's oldest and contemporary pyramids. After one false start in about 2660BC the hill was raised to one pre-determined plan